Teaching Economics Through Business Simulation Games

Table of Contents

Chapter 1. Introduction

Engage, strategize, and master the complex world of economics while having fun—sounds too good to be true? In this Special Report, we "Explore Teaching Economics Through Business Simulation Games." This report isn't just another dry read on economics; it's your gateway to a pioneering approach where understanding economic principles becomes an exciting venture! Designed for all, from educators seeking innovative teaching methods to avid learners looking for an interactive spin on economics, this report provides insightful, detailed exploration of how simulation games can revolutionize learning. What if learning economics felt less like a lecture and more like a game of Monopoly? Read on to dive into how this educational revolution is not just possible—it's already happening!

Chapter 2. Unmasking Economics: Traditional Teaching Methods

The traditional teaching of economics has typically revolved around a long-standing, systematic approach that involves textbooks, lectures, and the rote memorization of theories and facts. Where once this may have been the most effective mode of instruction, in a rapidly evolving world that thrives on agility and innovation, this age-old method is increasingly being called into question.

2.1. The Textbook Approach

A ubiquity in virtually all academic institutions, textbooks have long been the go-to resource for teaching economics. They offer a comprehensive and systematic approach to learning, with each chapter introducing a new concept, elaborately explained with definitions, diagrams, and sometimes real-world examples.

However, this model is not without its drawbacks. The inability of textbooks to foster an engaging, interactive learning environment often makes it difficult for students to grasp complex economic principles. Textbooks are one-sided conversations where information is handed to students without obtaining or guaranteeing their comprehension. This makes learning a passive process, where students consume information rather than actively engaging with it.

Another major limitation of textbooks is their static nature. Economic events, shifts, and policies are always evolving, but textbooks get outdated quickly and can't keep up with these rapid developments in real-time. Hence, they may fail in adequately preparing students to navigate the intricate dynamics of the real-world economy.

2.2. The Lecture Model

Following closely behind textbooks in their traditional usage are lectures. With this approach, professors deliver information verbally, often supplementing their speech with presentations or whiteboard diagrams. They serve as the primary source of knowledge, with students primarily playing passive roles, soaking in the information.

Lectures, akin to textbooks, also stifle student interaction. Albeit being a time-honored method of teaching, lectures tend to be monotonous, making it challenging to maintain students' interest throughout the session. Students might find it hard to follow complex principles and theories explained verbally, particularly when these are not supplemented with real-world examples or active teaching methods.

Further, lectures are generally static and linear, leaving no room for adaptive teaching. If a student doesn't understand a concept, it's tough to pause and clarify without disrupting the flow of the class or running out of allocated time.

2.3. The Problem of Rote Memorization

In the traditional educational system, rote memorization plays a significant role. As a skill, it's often useful when studying particular subjects, but when applied to economics, it can prove counterproductive. Economics is not a static field, with rigid rules; rather, it's a dynamic discipline with evolving theories and constant flux.

Rote memorization can also limit critical thinking. By focusing on studying to recall facts and theories verbatim for exams, students may miss understanding the underlying principles and their applications in real life. This confines their understanding within the realm of "bookish knowledge," restricting their ability to analyze, evaluate, and draw connections between economic concepts.

2.4. The Lack of Practical Exposure

One of the most significant gaps in traditional economics teaching methods is the lack of practical exposure. Theoretical learning, though essential, is insufficient without providing students the opportunity to apply concepts in real-world scenarios.

Practical exposure could be in the form of case studies that reflect real-world scenarios, internship opportunities, or simulations. Such experiences help students understand the practical applications of economic theories and concepts, preparing them better for future career paths.

2.5. Evolution is Needed

It's clear that traditional teaching methods in economics need a makeover. While textbooks and lectures may be useful to glean basic knowledge, there's a need to shift towards more interactive, student-inclusive, and practical methods.

The integration of modern teaching tools like business simulation games can help accomplish this. These interactive platforms can facilitate a stimulating learning environment, revealing the real-world dynamics of economics while enabling students to put theoretical knowledge into practice in a simulated, risk-free setting.

In the next chapters, we'll delve into how such simulation games can help reshape the future of economics education, providing students with a more engaging, practical, and comprehensive understanding of this critical field.

Chapter 3. The Convergence of Gaming and Education

With the advent of digital media, classrooms around the globe are witnessing a tectonic shift in the educational landscape. This change morphs the traditional style of education into a forward-thinking and innovative learning environment characterized by the integration of immersive technology - notably, games.

3.1. The Power of Gaming

In the last decade, gaming has evolved from a leisure activity to a potential learning tool. Unlike traditional learning methodologies, gaming is interactive nature, spotlighting active participation and engagement over passive absorption. For instance, consider a game of chess – it requires critical thinking, foresight, strategy, and the capability to predict opponents' movements. These skills are pertinent in a real-life context, emphasizing problem-solving and decision-making abilities.

When applied to education, gaming can promote an experiential form of learning, which is a stark contrast to the textbooks and prescribed syllabi that many education systems still adhere to. Learning through games can be stimulating, gripping, and personalized, tailoring instruction to individual strengths and weaknesses.

3.2. Immersive Learning Experience

Games create an immersive environment for learners. In the same vein as virtual reality, they transport users to an alternate, real-time scenario, instigating broadened perspectives and critical thinking. Business simulation games, for instance, can immerse learners in a virtual economic environment where they must navigate decision-making scenarios reflective of real-world conditions.

Games can also induce a sense of challenge, thereby motivating learners and leading to improved retention rates. This stems from the balance of skill and challenge – also known as the "flow" state. When learners are in this state, they are absorbed in their tasks, showcasing more involvement, effort, and productivity.

3.3. Translating Gaming to Educational Technology

Understanding the strength that lies in the gamified learning approach has led to a surge in educational technology or EdTech. Companies across various markets are aiming to incorporate gaming elements into their educational offerings. In the world of economics, applications like ECONland or Virtonomics offer educational content through intricate interfaces, allowing learners to apply academic concepts to real-world scenarios.

EdTech solutions that integrate gaming provide interactive learning opportunities, gradually replacing the monotonous, theory-heavy frameworks that have dominated education. Beyond direct academic application, these solutions leverage gaming to develop broader skills, like strategic thinking and problem-solving, often overlooked in traditional academic environments.

3.4. Implementing Gamification in Economics Education

Implementing game elements in economics can make the subject more interactive and comprehensible. Business simulation games can teach learners economic principles by assigning them the role of business owners or executives. For example, a player could understand supply and demand principles by managing stock levels in a virtual store, see the impacts of price elasticity through customer responses to price changes, and even learn financial skills like budgeting and forecasting.

Often, these simulated scenarios demonstrate the consequences of financial decisions and the influencing dynamics of a country's economy. This experiential learning approach thus effectively links educational understanding with practical knowledge – arguably, a more functional form of education.

3.5. Challenges and Future Prospects

Despite its immense potential, the adoption of gamification in economics education faces challenges. Schools and colleges may lack necessary resources or technical expertise; parents and educators may resist, fearing excessive game-time could distract from traditional study.

However, as technology evolves, so too does awareness about its potential in education. Stakeholders are gradually acknowledging the advantages of educational games. With continuing research and product development, we can expect further evolution and implementation of gaming-based learning tools. Furthermore, advanced technologies like artificial intelligence could personalize learning further, tailoring content to individual learners, thereby refining the learning process.

In sum, the convergence of gaming and education is a transformative venture that can revolutionize how economic principles are taught and understood. It stands at the intersection of fun and learning, creating an educational experience that is engaging, interactive, and meaningful.

Chapter 4. Business Simulation Games: An Overview

Understanding economic dynamics in a global context can be a daunting task. By orchestrating a sophisticated blend of supply chain management, market analysis, strategic decision-making, recognizing and adapting to financial fluctuations, and a plethora of other complex elements of economic theory, it becomes an intimidating endeavor. Thankfully, with pioneering advances in edutech, we now have business simulation games—interactive tools that simplify these concepts whilst providing a hands-on experience.

4.1. The Genesis of Business Simulation Games

In the trajectory of teaching economics and business, the advent of simulation games is a relatively recent development. Rooted in the advanced possibilities offered by technology, these games build upon traditional approaches, introducing a dynamic, interactive element in the educational journey.

Traditionally, classrooms—and even countries—relied upon a top-down economics teaching method where students passively received information, often struggling to grasp abstract concepts. However, the advent of the digital era brought about a paradigm shift, opening up possibilities for immersive, hands-on learning. It was in this crucible that business simulation games were born, designed to support, enhance, and invigorate the economic learning experience.

4.2. The Essence of Business Simulation Games

Business simulation games mimic real-world economic situations and market dynamics. They provide players with a safe platform to test various business strategies, learn from their mistakes, and understand the repercussions of their decisions—all in a controlled environment. These games typically feature different scenarios, from managing a small shop to running multinational corporations, allowing the players to address complex economic situations on a micro and macro scale.

Most business simulation games are built around scenarios that allow the player to take on the role of a business leader, with tasks and responsibilities designed to replicate actual economic challenges. These might include managing inventories, balancing supply and demand, adjusting prices, dealing with contingencies, and implementing strategic and tactical decisions under dynamic market conditions—bringing abstract economic concepts to life.

4.3. From Concepts to Practice

The potential of business simulation games in building economics cognizance rests on the ability to bridge theory with practice. Here we present a closer look at how these games translate to a significant learning experience.

1. *Active Engagement*: Instead of relying on passive absorption of facts, business simulation games encourage players to actively participate, innovate, strategize, and implement these strategies according to changes in a simulated marketplace, leading to high engagement levels that increase learning and retention rates.

2. *Real-World Application*: Business simulations provide a practical outlook on concepts taught in classrooms. They allow learners to

see theoretical concepts in action, providing them insights into how these concepts work in the real world.

3. *Instant Feedback*: These games offer immediate feedback on decisions made by participants. This instant gratification or rectification helps the learner adapt their understanding and improve their strategies in real-time.

4. *Risk-Free Environment*: Operating within a simulated environment allows learners the liberty to make bold decisions and errors without fearing debilitating consequences. This encourages exploration, discovery, and deeper understanding—a cornerstone for effective learning.

4.4. Integrating Business Simulation Games Into Education

Business simulation games cater to a wide range of learning environments, from schools and universities to corporate training programs. They can be incorporated into a curriculum in various ways:

- *In-class Activities*: Games can be used as part of regular course activities, allowing students to apply lessons practically.

- *Homework or Assignments*: Students can be tasked with achieving specific goals in a game as part of homework or assignments.

- *Extra-Curricular Activities*: Simulations can be used in business clubs or for economics-related events and competitions.

Instructors can monitor student performance within the game, provide feedback on their strategies, and tailor class materials based on areas where students struggle.

4.5. Conclusion

Undeniably, the ability to simplify intricate economic concepts into engaging, digestible formats is the real power of business simulation games. As they continue developing and expanding, their capacity to revolutionize economics education is unprecedented. They are not just computer games—they are robust learning ecosystems that nurture the understanding of economics in a way that aligns with the 21st-century learning ethos of interaction, engagement, and practical application.

Chapter 5. Economic Concepts Through Virtual Business Scenarios

The marriage of economics and technology has proven itself as a successful union, especially with the advent of educational simulation games. These virtual environments build a playground for business scenarios, making complex economic concepts accessible, engaging, and comprehensible. In this plunge into the digital realm, we'll explore how these games have amplified the teaching and learning experience, transforming theoretical abstract concepts into realistic ventures.

5.1. Equilibrium Price and Quantity in a Virtual Marketplace

Equilibrium price and quantity mark the point where supply meets demand. Teaching this concept traditionally would involve graphical illustrations. However, in a simulation, learners can experience the dynamics of supply, demand, and equilibrium in real-time.

Consider a 'Virtual Farmer's Market' simulation. Participants assume roles of farmers and customers. Each player as a farmer is tasked with producing and selling crops based on supplies, production costs, and market prices. Customers, on the other hand, have fixed budgets they must manage to feed their families. The ensuing transactions simulate a competitive marketplace, thus illustrating how prices naturally tend towards equilibrium.

Through this, players grasp and apply fundamental economics concepts, from consumer/producer surplus to the effects of shifts in supply and demand curves.

5.2. Monopolistic & Competitive Market Structures

Understanding the dynamics of market structures stands as a core tenet of economics. Let's travel to another game scenario, this time one that elucidates the conception of monopolistic and competitive markets.

'Virtual Business Tycoon' offers players the chance to manage rival companies in various sectors, determining prices, quantities, and marketing strategies. Through trial errors and informed decisions, players learn how monopolies can manipulate prices due to lack of competition, the implications of oligopolies, or how perfect competition leads to the lowest price for consumers.

5.3. Fiscal & Monetary Policies

Fiscal and monetary policies prove challenging for learners due to their abstract nature. But imagine a game that allows students to assume the roles of fiscal and monetary policymakers and tackle real-world economic issues! 'Virtual Central Bank' does precisely that.

Players, acting as central bankers, can adjust interest rates, stimulate lending, or control inflation. On the fiscal side, they control public spending and taxation policies, thereby experiencing the tug-of-war between inflation, unemployment, and public debt—a struggle that real-world policymakers encounter daily.

5.4. The Economy's Circular Flow

Comprehending the circular flow of an economy is essential, as it signifies the movement of goods, services, and money. With 'Virtual Island Economy,' students participate in an immersive island world where they get involved in various economic activities such as fishing, trading, and crafting.

Such activities illustrate the circular flow within a closed system, enabling students to observe and learn about economic leakages and injections, the roles of households, firms, and the government, and the importance of each in maintaining economic stability.

5.5. Behavioral Economics & Decision Making

Adding the 'Human Element' to economics, i.e., human behavior, decision-making, and cognitive biases, can often be challenging. A simulation game called 'Nudge' helps bridge this gap.

Players make various choices, undergo decision-making dilemmas, and observe how their actions influence not just their outcomes but also the game world at large. The game breeds an understanding of the often irrational behavior of economic agents, thereby providing a hands-on experience in behavioral economics.

Teaching concepts through such an experiential mode of education allows learners to gain deep, practical insights into otherwise hard-to-grasp, abstract economics theories. They 'do' rather than 'listen,' boosting their understanding and retention of economic concepts. As we move forward, the gamification of learning and teaching economics is set to transform not just the learning environment but also the learners themselves.

Chapter 6. The Role of Competition in Learning Economics

Just as the arteries of economic theory pulse with the force of competition, so too does this vital principle animate the exhilarating realm of business simulation games. Competition, an essential cornerstone in the field of economics, has deep-reaching implications for how individuals, firms, and nations interact. By integrating competition within the realm of simulation games, we can understand the intricate dynamics of market forces, price determination, demand-supply interactions, monopoly, and beyond, in an engaging and immersive milieu.

6.1. Understanding Competitive Markets through Simulation

Competitive markets are at the heart of any robust economy, acting as the arena where buyers and sellers interact to exchange goods and services. Simulating these market conditions can help us appreciate key economic principles. Business simulation games can mimic real-world competitive circumstances, from monopolistic competition to perfect competition. For instance, players can create virtual goods, determine prices, analyze consumer demand, and observe how competitors respond in different situations. This combination of artificial intelligence, user interface design, and economic theory provides an interactive platform for understanding the essence of competition in economics.

Having competition integrated into these games gives participants a hands-on, active learning experience. As players, they can dive into economic competition, testing strategies and decisions that would have tangible consequences in real-world scenarios. Will undercutting a competitor's price lead to increased market share, or will it ignite a price war that erodes profits? How do policies and market dynamics influence competitive outcomes? Through simulation, these theoretical concepts transform into testable hypotheses in an immersive learning environment.

6.2. Monopolistic Competition and Oligopoly in Detail

Monopolistic competition and oligopoly - these market structures permeate our economic reality but can seem abstract in traditional classroom settings. Business simulation games shine by bringing these concepts to life, offering the opportunity for players to engage with them directly.

When each player in the game sets up their own firm, they essentially create a monopolistic competition scenario. Each character is a single firm among many, offering a product slightly differentiated from the others—an ideal learning process for understanding price optimization, branding, and marketing tactics. Experience with monopolistic competition in this setting can be instrumental in grasping concepts such as marginal costs, average costs, and price discrimination.

Similarly, when the game narrows down to a few dominant firms controlling the market, it segues into an oligopoly. Players can witness firsthand how mutual interdependence leads to strategic decision-making, with each firm constantly watching and reacting to the others' moves. This offers a unique perspective on anti-competitive behavior and highlights the need for regulation and fair competition policies.

6.3. Leap from Theory to Practice: Competition Policy

Teaching economics through simulation games also offers a tangible way to understand and analyze competition policy — a critical area that safeguards the interests of consumers and businesses alike. Anti-competitive behaviors such as predatory pricing, collusion, or cartel formation and their harmful effects on the economy can be simulated. This allows players to recognize the significance of competition laws and learn the macroeconomic impact of regulation.

Through creating, applying, and overturning various policies within the game's microcosm, participants can appreciate the challenge regulators face in facilitating fair competition and market efficiency. This form of experimental learning encourages critical thinking and problem-solving about complex economic puzzles and public policy issues.

6.4. Competition Driving Innovation and Efficiency

Economics dictates that competition breeds innovation and efficiency—drivers of economic growth and prosperity. Business simulation games stage a creative battlefield where players can observe and experience this principle in action. As virtual firms compete for market share, they have to innovate, whether through improving their products, enhancing their processes, or developing novel marketing strategies.

Simultaneously, players learn the effect of competition on operational efficiency. Under the constant pressure of competition, businesses must seek to lower their costs and improve their production processes to survive and prosper. This dynamic, competitive environment fosters an understanding of crucial economic principles in a practical and engaging way.

In conclusion, business simulation games are a transformative tool, making intricate economic theories accessible, interactive, and enjoyable. The role of competition, when understood through this vivid lens, not only enhances the instinctual grasp of economic principles but also encourages a more profound and organic engagement with the subject matter. Teaching and learning economics has never been so exciting—welcome to the future of pedagogy.

Chapter 7. Enhancing Critical Thinking and Decision Making

Undoubtedly, one of the primary benefits that business simulation games offer is the enhancement of critical thinking and decision-making skills. This is achieved by immersing learners in scenarios that push for adaptive thinking, strategic planning, and practical execution of theoretical knowledge.

7.1. Interactive Learning Environment

Simulation games are designed to replicate real-world scenarios in a controlled, risk-free environment. In these virtual settings, learners are exposed to a variety of unpredictable situations that not only emulate real-life problems but also demand real-life solutions. These experiences allow learners to witness cause and effect relationships directly and learn from their own decisions. This first-hand experience, coupled with immediate feedback, accelerates understanding and facilitates the internalization of complex economic concepts.

7.2. Encouraging Problem-Solving

One of the core elements of these simulations is problem-solving. Players are tasked with working through various dilemmas that require them to understand and manipulate several economic parameters such as pricing, supply and demand, competitive landscapes, and other business-related variables. By familiarizing players with these concepts in an engaging, interactive way, the simulation games enhance problem recognition and problem-solving abilities. This experience effectively prepares learners to address real-world business and economic challenges.

7.3. Decision Making in a Safe Environment

Naturally, the decision-making process is fraught with the risk of failure. Often, the fear of failure can impede learners' confidence to make bold decisions. Business simulation games alleviate this fear by providing a safe space where learners can experiment, make mistakes, and understand possible repercussions without any real-life consequences. This trial-and-error tactic bolsters learners' confidence to make decisions, facilitating the growth of their problem-solving capabilities.

7.4. Developing Strategic Thinking

Economic-based simulation games also push participants towards developing long-term strategic thinking. They are designed to challenge players on multiple fronts, forcing them to think ahead and plan for future eventualities. Recognizing patterns, making predictions based on available data, managing resources efficiently and coping with scarcity are essential abilities that these games can cultivate.

7.5. Promoting Collaborative Learning

Depending on the nature of the simulation, economic-based games can also promote collaborative learning. Some games require learners to form teams, defining roles, dividing tasks and conjoining efforts to achieve shared objectives. These shared experiences encourage communication, cooperation, and negotiation skills. The critical thinking involved in coordinating resources and efforts towards a common goal is another substantial takeaway from these games.

7.6. Enhanced Understanding of Economic Theories

Let's sum it up, the interactive nature of simulation games transforms abstract economic theories into tangible concepts. By demonstrating relationships between different economic variables, the simulations help learners observe the ripple effects of their decisions. Visualization of abstract concepts helps solidify understanding and retention of knowledge.

Simulation games have to potential to revolutionize the learning experience of economics — transforming what's traditionally perceived as daunting and dry into something engaging and tangible. By fostering a strong foundation of critical thinking, decision-making, and strategic planning capabilities, these games equip learners to apply and extend classroom learning to real-world scenarios. Despite their playful exterior, business simulation games offer a profound and effectual learning experience, making them a pioneering pedagogical tool in economics education.

Chapter 8. Educator Perspectives: Success Stories from the Classroom

With business simulation games, teachers largely become the facilitators of learning, providing necessary guidance yet letting students make their own decisions, and learn from their outcomes. Successful implementation of these virtual games in classrooms has yielded exemplary educational accomplishments. Amassed here are few such triumphs that demonstrate the practical application, and effectiveness of economic games in stimulating an instinctive learning process in economics.

8.1. Teacher One: The Journey from Black-Board to Online Games

A seasoned economics teacher, Teacher One used to employ traditional economics teaching methods. One day, she stumbled upon the idea of business simulation games which piqued her interest. Initially skeptical, she introduced the games in her classroom with a careful structured approach. She started with simpler simulation games, utilizing them as a complementary tool, ensuring it doesn't override the basic learning methodologies.

As students began showing more interest and engagement, business simulation games gradually started gaining prominence in her classroom. Today, Teacher One's classroom is buzzing with active participation, engaging discussions and most importantly, active learning. The dramatic improvement in grades and overall student enthusiasm towards economics vindicates her innovative approach.

8.2. Teacher Two: Breaking the Monotony

Portfolios of real-world companies, market scenarios, diversified sectors, and economic cycles—business simulation games introduced by Teacher Two professed to offer more than just economics learning to her students. They were designed to break the monotony. To her, the most challenging part was not the implementation of the new approach, but to ensure student engagement during the transition. She feared losing the attention of her students during this phase, thus implemented the games in smaller intervals originally.

Her students quickly became engaged and curious. The game settings allowed them to compete, strategize and react to changing economic scenarios. They learned to take risks, understand the consequences and to strategize for future prospects. This real-time learning process significantly enhanced the students' grasp of economic concepts, decision-making abilities, and critical thinking skills.

8.3. Teacher Three: Building Future Entrepreneurs

Teacher Three had the vision to inspire his students to understand an economic entity from the standpoint of its entrepreneur. He envisioned creating a platform that lets students do more than just applying formulas and preparing outlines. Rather, he introduced simulation games to make them understand the influence and impacts of economic decisions on a business.

Results were stunning! Students began simulating their ventures, identifying market opportunities, and making strategic decisions. They learned about resource allocation and managing finances, all while encountering real-world challenges faced by entrepreneurs. This provided proof that learning economic concepts can be engaging, stimulating, and enjoyable.

8.4. Teacher Four: Empowering Independent Learning

The advantage of simulation games that appealed most to Teacher Four was the element of independent learning. She noted that students get to make sense of their mistakes—or their successful strategies—in real-time. They can observe the ripple effects of their decisions firsthand in a virtual risk-free environment, which immensely aids in shaping their learning curve. The increased understanding while they play out various economic scenarios is a testimony to the potent impact of these simulation games.

In summary, integrating economics teaching with business simulation games has shown evidence of guiding students towards a deeper understanding rather than rote learning. Observations show that students have emerged not just as successful learners, who understood the subject matter well, but also as confident individuals ready to embrace the real-world economic scenarios with analytical minds and creative approaches.

Achievements of these four educators are just a fraction of many success stories in classrooms due to the innovative approach in teaching economics using business simulation games. The revolution in learning economics is here, and as these educators showcase, it's effectively reforming the traditional approach one classroom at a time.

Chapter 9. Implementation Tips for Teaching Economics via Simulation Games

Teaching economics in an engaging and comprehensive manner is a formidable task, particularly in an era where human attention span is at a premium. Traditional lecture-based teaching methods often fail to motivate students, leading to low retention rates of important economic concepts. Therein lies the potential of simulation games as a pedagogical tool, which allows students to directly interact with and influence economic environments to aid their learning.

The following section provides detailed, in-depth strategies for utilizing simulation games to teach economics. It offers practical suggestions regarding the integration of simulation games in your curriculum and presents guidelines to monitor student progress effectively.

9.1. Choose the Right Game

The first step in incorporating simulation games into your teaching process is to carefully select a game that aligns with your course objectives. A range of economic simulation games are available in the market—each covering different economic topics and requiring varying levels of cognitive engagement.

Search for games that reflect the real-world economic scenarios you wish your students to explore. The game should be able to immerse players into market dynamics, corporate decision-making, or financial strategy—depending on your teaching goals.

The choice of the simulation game should also factor in the technical proficiency of your students, their age, and their familiarity with economic concepts. For instance, a high school economics class might benefit from a simpler, consumer-focused simulation game, whereas an MBA class may need a more complex, immersive business simulation.

9.2. Integrate the Game into Your Syllabus

Next, it's essential to thoughtfully intertwine the game with your syllabus to ensure that it augments the teaching process rather than acting as a standalone activity. Use the game as a practical tool to create a bridge between theoretical concepts and their real-world application.

Plan ahead on where to fit the game sessions in your teaching timeline. For some topics, it may make sense to use the game as an introductory tool, piquing students' interest before diving into the theoretical underpinnings. For other topics, the game could act as a platform to reaffirm and practice concepts already discussed in the class.

Consider assigning specific gaming tasks as homework, allowing students to experiment on their own. This prior gameplay can then be used as a groundwork for class discussions.

9.3. Provide Guidance

The use of simulation games in teaching economics—though highly interactive and engaging—can be confusing for students if not properly guided. Provide clear directions about the game's objectives, game mechanics, and scoring criteria before starting the game.

Discuss with students how the game integrates the economic theory they are studying. Make them aware of the correlations between the games' mechanics and the key concepts they need to understand.

Also, encourage them to ask questions whenever they face difficulties. This can help build a dialogue around the lessons learnt and stimulate critical thinking about economic policy and practice.

9.4. Facilitate Reflection

A crucial part of teaching economics via simulation games is to facilitate reflections after each game session. Post-game discussions can solidify their understanding as they interpret their gaming experience through the lens of economic concepts.

Frame questions that push them to not only reason out their actions taken during the game but also to apply their knowledge in analyzing the outcomes. For instance, if a student, playing as a business owner, decided to cut prices to beat competition – discuss not just the tactic but its potential impact from a larger economic perspective.

Such deep reflection helps in unraveling the nuances of economic theories and practice, fostering enhanced learning.

9.5. Monitor Progress

Tracking students' progress, while they are engrossed in the gaming environment, allows for real-time assessment of their understanding of theoretical concepts. This can be achieved by observing the decisions they make in the game, identifying patterns, mistakes or areas of struggle.

Some simulation games generate detailed analytics of players' actions, providing you with valuable data to gauge each student's cognitive strengths and weaknesses. Use this information not just for grading purposes but also to tailor your teaching methods and to provide personalized feedback.

Teaching economics through simulation games promises not just to be an entertaining experience, but also an academically enriching one. The prospect of implementing these games into your economics classes can seem daunting, but remember—like any game, once you start, you learn and improve along the way. Happy gaming!

Chapter 10. Pruning Potential Pitfalls in Game-Based Learning

While business simulation games offer a myriad of benefits for teaching economics, like any instructional tool, they pose potential challenges and pitfalls. Some of these challenges could undermine their efficacy if not effectively mitigated. In this regard, we'll delve into identifying and pruning potential pitfalls inherent in game-based learning, discussing strategies to best handle these issues, thereby maximizing the educational benefit of this innovative pedagogical approach.

10.1. Navigating the Complexity of Games

One of the common pitfalls in game-based learning is the complexity involved in gameplay. A learning game can sometimes be so intricate that players feel overwhelmed. This can end up obscuring the learning objectives and distract players from the core economic principles meant to be learned.

To mitigate this, educators can break down the gameplay into digestible stages, with each stage focusing on a particular concept. Students can be allowed to master one stage before proceeding to the next. Regular debriefings can also be beneficial to facilitate comprehension and reinforce the economic theories explored during gameplay.

When designing a game for an economics class, it's essential to ensure the complexity of the game aligns with the understanding level of the student. While high complexity games may work well for students with a solid foundation of basic economic concepts, they may present daunting challenges to novices.

10.2. Debunking the Myth of "Just a Game"

A common misconception often prevalent among learners when games are used for teaching is the notion that it's "just a game". Students could dismiss the learning opportunities available in the game and consider it only as a means of relaxation or entertainment.

To counter this, it's essential to create an environment that encourages learning and underscores the relevance of the game to the economics coursework. Educators should actively stress the correlation between the game and the course objectives, making it explicit that the game is an integral part of learning and assessment process.

10.3. Balancing Competition and Learning

Simulations games by their nature can become highly competitive. While competition can enhance engagement and motivation, excessive rivalry can overshadow the learning goals. It might lead to students focusing more on winning rather than understanding the core economic principles.

The key is to strike a balance between competition and learning. Educators can do this by rewarding understanding and application of economic theories over winning the game. Recognizing enlightening strategy formations, for instance, can be much more valuable than just acknowledging the ultimate winner.

10.4. Ensuring Engagement

Another potential pitfall in game-based learning is a lack of engagement. Not all students may find the same game equally appealing. Some might find it too challenging or too easy, which can hinder their learning process.

To keep engagement levels high, educators should strive for a versatile game design. The game should offer varying degrees of challenges, multiple pathways for success, and allow for different learning styles. Providing regular feedback can also help keep students motivated and engaged.

10.5. Addressing Technological Challenges

With the proliferation of digital business simulation games, technology can become both a tool and a challenge. Learners, particularly those unfamiliar with gaming technology, may struggle with mastering the game mechanics rather than absorbing the economic principles.

To combat this, consider incorporating a tutorial phase, where students are familiarized with gaming elements before diving into the core game. Providing ongoing tech support can also be invaluable, ensuring that students are not left struggling with tech issues instead of focusing on their economics learning journey.

Game-based learning offers a transformative approach to teaching economics. Nevertheless, potential pitfalls must be pruned to maximize the benefits. By appropriately addressing issues of game complexity, changing misguided mindsets, balancing competition with learning, ensuring engagement, and overcoming technological hurdles, we can harness the full potential of this innovative approach. Hence, we arm students with the knowledge to not only be successful in their economics class but also apply these principles in real-world scenarios.

Chapter 11. The Future of Economics Education: Simulation Games and Beyond

A paradigm shift has begun in the realm of economics education. With traditional pedagogical techniques proving less engaging for today's tech-savvy students, a unique, immersive, and interactive approach has come to the fore—simulation games. These games, by facilitating experiential learning, mimic real-world economic realities, lending a tangible facet to often abstract economic concepts.

11.1. Rise of Simulation Games in Education

In our digital age, simulation games are redefining the pedagogical landscape, ushering an innovative era of instruction that combines fun with intellectual rigor. Research shows that learning through simulations enhances the overall educational experience, as it boosts student engagement and fosters deeper understanding.

Simulation games provide a dynamic, interactive environment where learners engage in real-life economic issues, from managing a virtual business to ensuring smooth operation in a digital economy. These immersive experiences synchronize learning with entertainment, making arduous subjects like economics a child's play.

Enhancing problem-solving skills, decision-making, strategic thinking, and planning capabilities, while promoting collaborative learning, simulation games are proving instrumental in multidimensional learning, revamping the conventional classroom ethos.

11.2. Economic Simulations: In Action

Lecture-based courses often fail to stimulate learner involvement, thus impeding comprehension. However, simulation games turn this narrative on its head. They open a world where learners develop their economies virtually, trade, negotiate, strategize, and respond to economic shocks—experiencing the thrill and complexities of economic principles firsthand.

For example, 'SimCity' allows players to wear the mayor's hat and manage their city closely. They deal with issues such as taxation, zoning, public services, and more, mirroring real-life economic decision-making processes. Other games like 'RollerCoaster Tycoon' not only spark creativity but also teach intricate market dynamics, as players strive to make profitable theme parks.

11.3. Simulation Games and Experiential Learning

According to the proverb "tell me and I forget, show me and I may remember, involve me and I understand"; experiential learning—a cornerstone of simulation games— emphasizes "learning by doing." It enables students to apply complex theories to practice, leading to an intricate understanding of economics.

When applied to economics education, simulation games catalyze the development of vital skills such as critical thinking and decision-making. More importantly, they enable learners to see the consequences of their actions and strategies—be it bankruptcy or an economic boom—thus ingraining lessons more efficiently.

11.4. Challenges and Overcoming Them

However, the use of simulations in education is not without its challenges. Navigating the technical aspects of a game might be taxing for some, detracting from the learning experience. The solution lies in initial comprehensive tutorials and ongoing tech-support throughout the learning journey. The educator's role is also vital here, not as a conventional lecturer but as a facilitifier, a term combining 'facilitator' and 'certifier', guiding the learner's seamless transition into this brave new world of learning.

Chapter 12. Simulation Games: A Forecast into the Future

Much more than a passing trend, simulation games are here to stay. As artificial intelligence and machine learning permeate the sector, we can envisage more sophisticated simulation games mirroring real-time global situations, thus enriching the learning spectrum. Teachers too will likely employ AI analytics to gauge individual student progress, paving the way for personalized learning paths.

As we see, the future of economics education leaps beyond the bounds of traditional teaching, racing ahead to embrace a vivid amalgamation of technology and pedagogy. The interactive simulation games, emerging as primary teaching constituents are not just enlivening the economics learning canvas but sculpting the future of education—a future that promises to be more engaging, more collaborative, and indeed, more fun.

www.ingramcontent.com/pod-product-compliance
Lightning Source LLC
Chambersburg PA
CBHW072223290526
45794CB00007B/2860